The H

Messages from Within

by
Jenessa Qua

The Healing: Messages from Within

Copyright 2018 © Jenessa Qua

The moral right of the author has been asserted.

First Printed in United Kingdom 2018

Published by Conscious Dreams Publishing
www.consciousdreamspublishing.com

ISBN: 978-1-912551-34-7

Dedication

Dedicated to all those who feel the heavy heart. Release and step out of the darkness allowing your true healing love light to shine once more.

Acknowledgements

Special thanks to:

♥ My wonderful son and family for all their love and support;

♥ Christine, Cos, Norberta, Laurence, Sharon, Michelle, Nazneen, Jo, Amir, Edward, Belinda, Toni, Valerie, Paul, Jenny, Lai, Gee, Colin, Joyce and Leanne;

♥ Danni and all the team at Conscious Dreams Publishing;

♥ Organisations that helped me on my journey:

- The Havens
  www.thehavens.org.uk
  02032996900

- The Woman and Girls Network
  www.wgn.org.uk
  08088010660

- Transformation Powerhouse
  www.transformation.gs
  020 8472 1800

- One in Four
  www.oneinfour.org.uk
  020 8697 2112

Contents

Introduction

I had a mad writing splurge on Saturday night. Went to bed 5am! Then today I had this overwhelming feeling. It was so bizarre. I was in the middle of getting dressed and felt compelled to instantly go to my computer and start typing frantically like a half-naked mad woman possessed.

I really don't know what is going on or why this is happening to me, but feel I must accept whatever it is with open arms. I will try to go with the flow and if I can, somehow try to find the meaning of it all.

I emailed the above to a friend two days after it all started.

It was January 2012 and, initially, this is how my writing began. The words were written by me, but somehow through a kind of opening of my subconscious mind.

Whenever the feeling came, day or night, I'd just type before I had actually fully formed the sentences in my head. Many times, I'd be so tired I'd touch type away on my laptop with a nodding head and closed eyes. On several occasions, I had to leave my bed to release the build-up of words. There was no brain capacity left to memorise them as they flooded into my mind like a speedy dictation. It got so bad that when absolutely exhausted, I'd rest my head on the back of my hands as my fingers translated the magic.

I would look up and read the new offering with amazement. The wonderful words were so strange but at the same time familiar to me. I eagerly awaited the next episode. It became frightening as some of the verses were so 'out there', I couldn't understand how this had come from me.

I wrote 20 poems in seven days. Being a singer songwriter, I wished I could write fantastic songs that quickly. That would be a dream! I found it incredible that I should find myself writing so many lyrics with no melody. In a way, I feel the verses do sing a tune in recognition of my inner truth.

Each piece took me on another adventurous ride. I felt uplifted and joyous. Tears of happiness filled me and sometimes sadness at all the injustice and heartache in this world forcing me to consider in what way I'd be able to contribute to a positive change, that would somehow, maybe one day make even a small difference.

Since this phenomenal awakening, I have taken on writing from the heart birthing the silent whispers of my inner thoughts and feelings. My mission is to tackle various topics and experiences that have impacted my life.

As an introduction to my writing, I'd like to share with you my journey, which began in 2012, in the form of my short story Slimspiration which was first published in 2017 in an anthology Love Unboxed 2. This is in three parts, preceding the poetry chapters.

Each chapter has their own individual identity. In Beauty, feel the magical wonder of life, love and nature. Let it take you on a deep appreciation of the simple things which make your smile within.

Strength, brings an insight into challenges faced when dealing with trauma and negative thinking. Growing from a fragile state of mind to learning resilience.

The true core essence of transforming is demonstrated in Rise. You will find uplifting empowerment of self-love, belief and encouragement with pure gratitude in appreciation to the highest element divine within.

I do not profess to follow any particular religion as such, but have always had an open mind to the spiritual side of things. I only know what I personally feel which is we are part of and the embodiment of the living Universe and that God resides within us all. I know I am still in the infancy stage of my awakening and in time hope to comprehend its full meaning for me and what effect, if any, it may have on the world.

Producing this book is a small but personal contribution I felt I should gift to others. By revealing these aspects of my life, I hope this conscious giving of me will show that you are not alone in difficult times.

Life has many ups and downs and we are blessed with a kaleidoscope of emotions to match. It's OK to not be 'OK', but don't suffer in silence. Sometimes you may feel that no one in the world understands you, or could possibly know what you are going through. Give yourself a break and try to nurture a kind and loving self. You are worthy and deserving of a good life. Permit yourself to release your fears, seek positive supports and outcomes to let your light shine.

So take in my secret journey of intimate words to another plane. Let it comfort and inspire you. Each piece is precious to my heart. May you be transformed and touched to your soul.

Universal Blessings,
Jenessa.

SLIMSPIRATION ♥ PART 1

*"Whether you think you can or you can't,
either way you are right."*

Henry Ford
1863–1947

TIME TO LIVE

You cannot hear me
The silent scream inside
Can't know how it feels
To want to run and hide
From the pointing stares
And the shock in their eyes
The sniggering laughter
At my enormous size

Not about how much
Or how little I do eat
As deeper is my hunger
Wanting to feel complete
For it is just the symptom
Many years of the denial
I use as my protection
From more tears and trials

The constant contradiction
Forever fighting self
First loving then the loathing
My poor emotional health
Fresh new start is needed
Emerge from my cocoon
Like a beautiful butterfly
For me to truly bloom

A totally blank canvas
To rewrite and explore
Add awesome vibrant colours
To worship and adore
Time to take the challenge
Must be ready for the fight
Conquering my demons
To strive for better life

Growing Up

'A how you look big so?!' In his laughing Jamaican voice, that was my dad's greeting words when I got home from school. I was used to his negative remarks. As usual, I pretended not to hear. It was day three of not eating any food, (apart from an apple) in an attempt to reduce my large bust. So on this occasion, his words stung. Life had always been difficult at home in my large family. My twin brother and I were the youngest born of nine children, including two sets of twins.

Growing up in the 70s was a mixture of good, bad and traumatic times. I don't remember much about my childhood; especially the younger years, as most of it I subconsciously blocked out. There were a couple of nice memories, but unfortunately the bad ones far outweigh the good. I was never sure of myself and felt confused and insecure, but mostly unlovable. It wasn't always easy to be heard amongst all my siblings. Although they'd say my brother and I were often treated like babies and spoiled. I learnt quickly how to get attention by being a good girl which resulted in getting rewarded with extra food treats. I think that's when my distorted connection with food must have begun. When I did do something bad, it was frightening punishment with heavy licks from my strict father's belt.

Even more painful to witness, was the terrifying beatings my poor mother endured from a violent controlling husband. I would overeat to comfort myself, from living in the tense atmosphere of being on edge most of the time. Not knowing when or what the next explosive argument would lead to. I dreaded familiar sounds of tumbling, crashing, shouting and crying screams from my mother.

At school, I was able to escape from all the madness at home. I loved singing and dancing but felt awkward and different. Although I hated bringing attention to my large body, my school dance class gave me great joy of expression. At 12 years old, I had bigger breasts than all the girls in school and hated wearing my awful 'Doreen' by Triumph, 34DD cup bra. Through my teens, I continued to eat my way through depression. A few years later, I discovered boys, or more accurately, they discovered me. I had my first boyfriend at age 15; he didn't seem to mind that I was fat. It was great at first but didn't last long as when my father found out. That was the end of that. He was actually brave enough to come to my house to ask him if he could take me to a concert he'd bought tickets for. Of course, my father responded with a big fat 'NO!' I always thought I was undeserving and unworthy of love. So from then on, if I was ever lucky enough to have another boyfriend I'd do everything I could to please and keep him. The heartache of losing that first love hit hard and I began eating more to soothe the pain. Life was horrible. I couldn't wait to leave home, finally breaking out from the hell my father created aged 17.

Chapter 1:
Beauty

Feel the wonder of joyous beauty in your life
Let it fill you with bliss

Prayer

I ache with heartfelt tears of joy by your presence in me. How am I worthy of such splendour and anointment? An insignificant speck of dust compared to your enormity. Thank you for my wonderful life and another blessed day on this earth plane. I have so much to be thankful for. Your love is pure and divine; I am filled with contentment and thankful for every hour daily. So grateful, I am overwhelmed with emotion. I walk in your grace dear one, feeling your spirit within my higher self and am truly humbled. Blessings! ♥

IN THE REIGN SHINE

The prayer chakra of the inner voice guides the way
Hear the enlightenment bell resonate the sound
Piercing through your third eye filling up your well
Grateful evermore in the power you now feel

All consuming love is the way that you reveal
Holding the quintessence so elite you are delirious
Every cell in your body now vibrating in sync
Beauty affection of life so cherished and meek

Wonder no more in the emptiness cold and alone
Time has come for you to make your arrival known
Giving all your glory in luminous colour vision
For the blind to see and feel the majestic wisdom

In the reign shine you are purified and lush
No longer in mono but digital surround sound
With perfect precision you are now in tune
To echo the supreme love to shower onto all

BEAUTY AND ELEGANCE

Vibrant and colourful, beautiful scented angels
So wonderfully perfect and pure in every way
Many variations peppered everywhere to see
Sent from heaven with love to bring us joy

From young buds we look to them with anticipation
Watching the slow steady growth as they sway
Dancing in the breeze alone, or with their siblings
Then we see slight colour suddenly peeking through

Multiple layers tightly wrapped around each other
As if hugging to keep warm in sleep before waking
To spread out individually within a family in unison
Glorious, they show themselves worshiping the sun

Their angel wing petals so fragile and delicate
Heads facing in all directions displaying their finery
Tubular steams holding them strong from the root
Or prickly bush with thorns to hurt you for disturbing

Mesmerized by fragrances intoxicating to inhale
That gives you such a warm glow feeling inside
Delivering immense happiness to all the senses
Blessed are we to be in their elegant presence

I REALLY DO CARE

While you were away, surprised I missed you so much
Pined for you, your smile, your laughter, and wonderful touch

Funny how you sometimes don't realise the massive effect
Another has on your life, only notice when they've left

Seems a part has somehow slightly shifted within you
A vanished rainbow captivating precious moments new

Brings a smile to you to see the awe of colour in sight
Moving is the heartfelt joy of beautiful soul light

Feels so good to show your dear loved ones you really care
Let them know without them in your life, you could not bear

BEYOND INFINITY

You are the sunshine in my night
A burning candle lighting the way

Let me drench myself deep
In your soulful power rays

Washing me pure and clean
With flawless diamond clarity

Refreshed I am lifted high
Levitated beyond infinity

You are the soul in me
And I in you we are entwined

The tread of a hemp rope
Twisted thick holding strong

To thee I do totally belong
As one we are the universe

COME TO THE LOVE LIGHT

Have I really opened up my soul for all to see?
Displaying my wealth in all its untold glory

Never before shown the trueness of my worth
I offer myself to all so they too may be nude

Believers acknowledge the purity essence
Those still lost, mock with their human eyes

Ego vanished; the core spirit will arise from source
Brilliance and clarity of divine love is revealed

If you are willing, you too can also join the fold
But you'll have to sacrifice all you know to be

The false identity you have masked yourself in
All thoughts and feelings you deemed real

Come home to your magical kingdom afresh
Reborn in your soul instinct that navigates you

Of such greatness, you could not even fathom
Ascension beyond the cosmos to infinity

Not all will surrender to the seduction of my call
But will still be showered with the love light I beam

LOVING GRACE

Tears of joy, tears of sadness
At the need of a love so great
Oh how I long for someone
With a true and pure heart

Solely for me, my one and only
Who knows me inside out
What I'm really all about
And loves me just the same

The man I can cherish wholeheartedly
Knowing that we're so perfectly matched
Our souls blended as if completely one
Strong, like magnetic forces drawn together

How I dream of the magnificent heart and soul mate
That I know the one and only divine has made for me
Will our paths cross, will we recognise each other?
Sometimes wonder if we are to see that day arrive

I pray our meeting point has not already gone
In the many years I denied myself love, even for self
Shutting out the pain from others who hurt me so
Never wishing to open that reoccurring wound again

Pray it's not too late, did our chance really pass us by?
Hope to see your face and welcome you open armed
Knowing that at last we take our rightful place
With each other's heart and in loving grace

YOUR SOUL LIGHTS THE WAY

Will this be the day I fly back home to where angels lie?
As a swirling kite accelerating in a cloudless sky

I long for my essence to be free from Earth's condition
With stars and galaxies my universal light glistens

Blissful the exhilaration of my soul ascension
Other ways don't satisfy no need to even mention

I try fully to express my inner vision on this plane
But see mystified faces when I say from which I came

Such lack of understanding and ridicule I receive
A multitude of religions is now what humans believe

Cannot see ultimately all having the same thread
Karma will return to you of which you lay your bed

Take off the mortal body coat for you to truly be
Restoring back to love and life your core for all to see

THE RECALL

Man child is coming to me
Do not forsake me in my last breaths
As I feel death near, hovering over
Ready to whisk me away to the surreal

I feel the weightlessness of my spirit preparing
See the rapid visual of my full and happy earth life before me
Mind thoughtful as I ponder on each precious moment
In humble gratitude and joyous love I will depart

Did I do good whilst I was here?
Were there people I touched with my presence?
So hope I will not be too sorely missed
Wonder if my purpose was met

Is my life's mission complete, or shall I return once again?
Turning over another leaf to emanate what is to be
Circling forevermore in the twists and turns of existence
I am ready for the end and the recall to the beginning

Let it be said that I was a willing party to it all
The highs and lows, mistakes and triumphs
I take ownership of the choices and decisions I made
Knowing each one was right for my journey of truth

PURPLESSENCE

Forever purple love
You are the glove
That warms my heart

Consumes my soul
With the deepest
Of pure divine

The glow is mine
In sunshine smile
Radiates the joy

I am enthralled
By your capture
Hold me close

Do not release
This vibration
Ecstasy to my core

Violet is the rain
Which you pour
To quench my root

The essence vapour
Rising from my crown
Sweet like honey dew

I breathe deep
For recirculation
Embrace to infinity

ME TIME

I soak in the hot fragranced water
Soothing away the stress and strain
As I melt in a dreamlike state

The steam mist so delicate in the air
Making the bright candle glow soft
Like an out of focus camera lens

Barely audible is the popping of bubbles
Luxurious foam floats on the surface
Envelops my body like an attentive lover

Tears of condensation roll down the tiles
As if rushing to join me in the grandeur
This time is mine alone I cut out the world

Splashing around as if a child at play
I then slide under and immerse myself
Instantly sensing the joy of womb return

Skin shining wet like an onyx statue
Content so pleasing is my 'Me' time
Long I stay wishing it will not end

Subsiding temperature tells me it's time
I must lift myself from the weightlessness
To again face reality and the demands of life

FEEL THE LOVE TOUCH

Do you see the real me?
The one I always hide
With big smiles and laughter

The child inside
Who needs a tender hug
And longs to be loved?

I see you and feel your soul
The pain you don't reveal
And keep at bay to save your heart

We choose to withdraw
Encased emotions too afraid to give away
Once so open, but now closed to feel the touch

To truly accept a real and pure love
Would mean total surrender
Could never allow in our tainted spirit

Instead we look outside to feel
Don't hear our inner voice saying it's OK
To love what and who we are

So blinded that we cannot see
The mirror reflection that makes us whole
Searching for the same vision we are one

Frightening to completely let go the fear
And have faith that we won't get hurt
But that is what we must do

Individually and for each other
Supporting even if on different paths
To expose the loving light in the world

TO MOVE IN TIME

Today I danced; I danced
To a funky tune on the kitchen radio
In my head I was the choreographer
Working out the video routine

Felt so good to move my body
To the beat in a new creative way
Oh how I love to dance,
The flow of movement stretching muscles

My heart racing in tempo
Like the rhythm of an African drum
Twist, turn, jump and spin
Bringing beads of sweat to my face

Exhilarated by the pure emotion
Rising my passion with excitement
By dancing I'm closer to God,
My spiritual frequency heaven sent

To sing, to feel, to move and dance
With such spellbound expression
Only angels feel the same freedom
When spreading wings for flight

Blissful pleasure to have that inner seed
Flourish and blossom out of you
Will always be a great love of mine,
As when I dance, I feel my glory shine

FLOWERS OF BEAUTY

I keep the beautiful dead flowers in the vase
As if frozen in time by liquid nitrogen

A visual reminder of how wonderfully precious
Yet so short life can be for every living thing

Air fragranced by their intoxicating sent now faded
Only close inspection reveals a slight hint of decay

How I miss the vibrant colours so vivid to my eyes
The fresh and delicate velvet soft petals cool to touch

Head now bowed as if in humble surrender at death
Slumbered with face down, but once so erect and proud

Yes, not normally the sight for a centrepiece on display
But find I learn great lessons from this oddity of mine

You may ask why not instead have decorative artificial ones?
To constantly capture the magnificent beauty forevermore

Of course that might be the easiest and best option to take
However, somehow I feel it would not convey nature's true reality

So forgive me if you find my mindset a little strange or morbid
That I should often keep beautiful dead flowers in my vase

FEED ME

I love the way you feed my soul
I'm satisfied, full to bursting point
Want to explode dispersing my pleasure
Like trillions of stars in the galaxy

So intense is the feeling of such joy
Don't think I've ever felt this way
Touching me deeply that I lose control
All consuming emotions pure and divine

My gratitude immeasurable
Never before cried wonderful tears
Many blessings I have been given in life
Will nurture and treasure, not squander

For it would be a sin to not appreciate
The glory, more precious than gold
Cannot be assessed, priceless in value
Only you can bestow this love supreme

AT LAST

I fly through the porthole ever ready for my command
Willing to embark on the uplifting that I know will follow
My soul stirring in a whirlwind of elation as a grateful being

The colours fill me with a tingling sensation in the frequency
Even with my eyes closed I see and feel their beauty aura
Radiating my spirit and body shell to another state sublime

I rise high now with the stars, penetrated with deepest love
Nothing can describe this, as comprehension not possible
Only heavenly angels hear my song and harmonize with me

Pleasure of the highest level, so intense I do not want to return
Earth has nothing for me now, as I have come home at last
But alas, my work is not complete for I have much to do still

Will I be understood when I tell of the riches that awaits us?
Inexpressible in earthly terms as one has to see for oneself
Who will take the first steps towards total soul contentment?

Are they ready? Am I ready, to show them the glory that's in store?
I pray I am worthy to let your love shine through me onto them
Carrying them with a heart overflowing with infectious love

To the realm of upmost happiness, not ever found before
Surely they would welcome having such a treasure inside
Knowing that it holds everlasting eternal peace at last

CHERUBS OF LOVE

Direct from source is the pure love connection
It flows through every living thing

Touches the soul uplifting the core spirit
The true essence of our whole being

Wondrous and inviting it beckons us to partake in its entirety
In the warmth of a forgiving coat we are generously clothed

Some fall under the spell, whilst others repel it
Choosing to follow a different path in cold dark clouds

But the rain still washes and cleanses them
Renewing to once again make a choice

To step into the sunshine of love and healing light
Glowing from the inside reaching out to others

Smile so wide for the deep felt happiness it brings
Eyes diamond bright with hypnotizing sparkle

You too can join the fun in the parade of life
Like infectious laughter on a spinning carousel

Feel the beautiful childlike innocence again
Returning as one in our angelic purity once more

IN PEACE AND LOVE

I'm on the edge of the gateway
To another time and space
On such a high, wondering
What delights will bestow me
I walk through with an open heart
And faith in the unknown

Feeling the effervescences of life
Overtake my whole being
Floating in the magnitude
Of you shining through me
All consuming blissfulness,
At one with source

Elated tears I cry with wonderful gratitude
For the experience
No other can bring me to this levitation
Of greatness and royalty
Glowing among the universal stars
As my armour of dexterity

Aligned at the precise position of full glory
For my life purpose
I glow with brilliant light illuminating
Every corner of the earth
My ray beams on every living thing
Giving hope and knowing

Suddenly captivating sounds of pleasure
Are heard
Voices raised high in praise
For the glorious blessing
Fulfilling the needs of plenty,
Now at peace with their soulfulness

What is this feeling you may ask?
Why it is deep penetrating heartfelt love
Love that was given to you at birth,
But wounded by your human coat
When you are able to show your true inner beautiful self,
Pure love remains

For we have forgotten ourselves
And the true purpose we were sent here
To learn, love, share, care, honour, respect,
Nurture, befriend and uplift
Within you is the gift of life and giving,
Do so with pure heart in peace and love

RELEASE MY ACHING HEART

I wish you would hold me in your arms and never let go
That is how my aching heart longs so much for you
Desire like I've never felt for anyone before
Overwhelmed my heart stops whenever I see your face

I try to remain calm and indifferent on the outside
But a fire ball of emotions burn within me
Once again I simmer my feelings
And pray my mask does not slip revealing the truth

Of me wanting to give you all of myself
Wishing you would see me as I see you
The one that captures me totally
I'm utterly besotted and obsessed

I wonder how long I'll have to keep up the pretense
Will I crack under the ever growing strain?
Or will you release me from this agonizing pain
With a passionate kiss from your beautiful lips

God knows why you have caressed my heart so deeply
I feel such an all-consuming love for you
Your presence in my life seems so vital
As if you are the air I inhale

At times I glimpse a spark of hope in your eyes
But know you are afraid to take that stride
The risk too great of spoiling what we already share
A connection as if twin souls once lost now reunited

Could it really be that we were only ever to be friends?
I find that so hard to believe and unable to bear
But that I will, just to have you near me
Even if only for a short while

ARE YOU READY FOR SO MUCH LOVE?

I need a love; I want a love to hold me in his arms
To make me feel as if I'm the sole reason he breaths
Like I'm the very oxygen he cannot live without

The one who cherishes me like the Queen I know I am
And I'll adore him as the loving King I know he is
Like the sea and the sand joined together always

Pure raindrops from heaven are the tears of love I feel
The warmth of the sun is the glow that is in my heart
Breeze on my skin is the gentle touch when we caress

Float on a cloud as you look into my moonshine eyes
Draws you closer to the twinkling stars in my galaxy soul
We swim in the pool of our cosmic ocean, an organic love

Eternal sweetness in the honey pot of gold in our rainbow
Overflowing in the love vibration that will penetrate us
Co-dependent and addicted to our ravishing thrust

Let me be the one that is yours alone and you mine
The time is long but wait I will, as I know you're worthy
The immense love I have to give, are you truly ready?

WE ARE LOVE

I love you
With all that I am
My entire being

A deep feeling so pure and true
My whole soul levitates
From your luminous love energy

We are one, connected
A core strength knowing no bounds
Beauty would not come close to describe

Our flow radiating from source
An essence of warmth I've never known
Comfortably nurturing my spirit

I am in you, as you are in me
We are one together in sync
Two souls in unison heart

We beat the rhythm of life
The universe itself
In our eternal existence

SLIMSPIRATION ♥ PART 2

"Our deepest fear is not that we are inadequate. Our deepest fear is that we are powerful beyond measure."

Marianne Williamson

Adulthood

The following adult years was explored with naïve eyes. I was inexperienced in the world and continued my comforting affair with food, to deal with responsibilities and stresses of solo life. I studied dance for two years at college, and moved into a co-op community house for ten people. I never made it as a dancer. That world was far too body conscious for my size, where I stood out way too much. I then took various retail and office jobs, but the mundane reality of 9 to 5 couldn't stimulate my senses. Instead, it fueled the empty loneliness I felt inside. By age 24, I had enough of my weight and foolishly tried slimming tablets. It cost me ten days observation in hospital, after collapsing with erratic heart palpitations. The family was supportive and my mother was truly grateful I was still alive, after previously losing one of my sisters, from the result of a negligent hospital procedure. Having dropped so much weight in a matter of weeks, my never ending abuse of food expanded my body further on return home.

I never had any male friends, always felt shy and awkward around them. We seldom mixed with boys in my small circle of girlfriends. When they approached me with complimenting advances, their interest melted my heart. My size never seemed to bother them, and the attention made me feel special. The next five years saw a few short term boyfriends come and go. I was fat and unattractive, that's how I thought of myself. Very insecure and eager to please, so grateful to have someone I thought actually loved me. At age 29, after what I thought was a wonderful holiday romance, I returned home to find I was pregnant. He had no interest whatsoever in my predicament, and I never saw him again. I was stunned, disappointed and angry at myself. How could I let this happen? Just two days later, I had the shocking blow of my mother passing away, the only person that truly loved me. Life would never be the same again.

I couldn't tell you what it felt like being pregnant as I was in total shock and denial the whole time. The devastation of losing mum was overwhelming. Having an unplanned child by a guy I hardly knew, who didn't want anything to do with me, was mind boggling. I was in complete turmoil and didn't know what to do. My emotions were all over the place and the pressure of it all sent me spiraling out of control into a breakdown. I had a healthy baby boy and, with the support of my family, I managed to get through the ups and downs of parenthood to raise a wonderful son. I loved him dearly, but hated myself, how I looked and felt. I never did properly grieve for my mother. It now seemed like I had no one in the world; apart from my little boy who gave me unconditional love. I felt very alone, with food my only faithful companion. I had no time for anything as my child was now number one on the list. I neglected myself terribly and my health and wellbeing suffered. I ignored the signs for years, until my poor food choices, lack of exercise and heavy weight resulted in Type 2 Diabetes.

Chapter 2:
Strength

Many painful challenges broke you
Yet you still survived to stand tall

BREAK THE CYCLE

How could you hit her, the one you claim to love so much?
Afterwards saying sorry, always thinking that's enough
Doesn't make it better, like soiled clothes clean from the wash
Bruises may not be displayed, a wounded soul now lost

Did you really have to force her, degrading her that way?
Upper hand you thought you had, the power games you play
Stayed with you for years to keep a promise said in faith
But couldn't do it once you put the black eye on her face

Wondered who'd be next in line to get the vicious treat
Might be daughter, two years old, that crawled at her own feet
Once your self-esteem and self-respect has almost gone
Extremely hard to take courage to leave and become strong

No question of not leaving all the terrain of abuse
Need to do it now before your neck is in a noose
Got to stop the cycle the pain you will not miss
Seeing parents shout and fight instead of tender kiss

The Healing Messages from Within | Jenessa Qua

A BRAVE MOTHER

When he shouted at her
She took it, but sometimes shouted back

When he belittled and humiliated her
She bit her tongue, then would lash him with it

When he questioned her sanity
She was silent, but questioned it herself for staying

When he deceived her with lies
She held on to her truth and faith

When he filled his eyes with hate and rage
She closed hers with love and prayer

When he overwhelmed her with sadness
She hid it from us and smiled to give us joy

When he blocked her way at every turn
She made a way with what little she earned

When he brutalised her with his hands
She shielded not herself, but us from her bruising

When he made her cry
She wiped her tears with the love for her children

When he forced her down with his power
She took all her strength to get up

When he was broken and blue
She licked his wounds and cradled him

When he felt life's strain and gave up
She took the wheel with courage and dignity

When you have been struck down repeatedly
It takes a brave woman to make him leave

I AM THE BROKEN DOLL

Did you hear me?
When I cried inside
Did you hear me?
In your monster disguise
When you hurt me
With controlling eyes
And deserted me
With your awful lies

When you touched me
Did you feel my fear?
My confusion
As you seemed so dear
Was not clear to me
Something wasn't right
In my childhood mind
You were protecting me

As any parent would
To keep from harm
But you stole my trust
Innocence alarmed
As the years moved on
I came to understand
What you did to me
Made you not a man

You're now weak and old
Seem so meek and mild
Not the towering giant
I grew to love and hate
I too am older
But still child in mind
As I shut out the world
To my grief and hurting

I try so hard
To live life right
But failure is the way
Things seem to turn out
Always holding back
Not trusting the real me
Feeling so worthless
Of one truly loving me

Over the years
I have rebelled
Not caring for self
Or seeing my wealth
And letting others
Demand on me
Sensing I was so
In need of love

To a few men
I have given
My entire soul
Showered with love
Hoping they too
Would give their all
Not knowing the dread
I instead caused

Never ending cycle
Of harm and abuse
I inflict on myself
Punishment for being bad
What else must I be?
For you to show such cruelty
To the one you made
Was it with love in your eye?

RIDE THE STORM TO THE OTHER SIDE

Why do the same old insecurities keep coming back?
Flooding my mind like a virus eating away the self-love

I've tried so hard to make it to a better place
But the reoccurring demons wake up to feed on me

I pray the invasion is short lived as I will myself to stand strong
With sword in hand to slay the multi-headed dragon of despair

Will have to take courage and fight with all my might
To regain the strength and greatness of my higher self

Once more I recognise the emotional inner pain I feel
Although hard to fully realise the meaning of its existence

The gathering storm seems to strike my soul like lightning
Tears fall in a constant stream, uncontrollable breath gasping

Never ending is the hurting as even when all is calm on the surface
That niggling sense of uncertainty lays waiting to suddenly ravage

Some say incurable as never really vanishes from your psyche
Will just have to whether the storm 'til I climb from the deep valley

THE BEAST OF PENGE EAST

My hands are shaking as I type
My stomach is turning over
I want to throw up so badly
I feel the salt water rise in my mouth

I spit it out into my cereal bowl
Disgusted with myself, I cringe
Then the nauseous feeling starts again
I try to hold it down before it erupts like a volcano

My mind hurts from the flashback terror
Nose running I blow away the slime
And feel so ill I spit out again and again
Wanting to eliminate the sick coming up now

What the hell is happening to me?
The emotional trauma still in my psyche
Like an invisible demon terrorising me
A damaged memory opposite to distant healing

The total shock of seeing that face
Why did I have to see his photo in my phone?
I feel numb; I start to blow and rock back and forth
As my body mimics that awful deep pain inside

I suddenly forget all the calming techniques
From countless therapy sessions I sat in
Trying to think of my special word, 'Beach'
As I zoom to fight or flight mode in 0.1 of a second

Shocking! The sight of him standing high and mighty
That smug arrogant smile on his face
With his female companion proud beside him
I wonder if she knew he was a vile monster

I forgot I saved his disgusting image
I so want to press delete, but I must fight that urge
It's identification evidence for the prosecution
Then everyone will know he's The Beast of Penge East

STOP LIVING THE LIE!

Living the lie, living the lie
Why do we breathe in the wicked lie?

We are surrounded with the bare truth everywhere
Open your eyes and look through the camouflage to see

For it is there as sure as the nose on your face
Evidence so clear but minds closed to acknowledge

So sickening is the daily delusion of false reality
Must purge and erase it from your belief system

Overtaken by the brainwash, you smile and laugh without a care
Whilst others sacrifice for justice and die to show you the truth

The scaremongering is totally setting fear and hate into us
We scatter and selfishly divide ourselves from each other

Forgetting we are brothers, one human race in life together
All different but made from the same divine quilt of love

Let us not believe the lie and take warm shelter in that quilt
Feeling the protective cover of pure love and trust in one another

Holding hands together in unity without judgement and ego
Freeing our world from contamination of greed and hatred

It starts with you and me, each one of us taking courage
To stand up for what we know is truly right in our very soul

Eliminate what is bad and wrong with fairness and truth
Is that not that the world you'd rather live in instead of the lie?

LOVE LIFE NOT LUST

DO NOT BLAME ME! For your uncontrollable desire
My beautiful womanliness, your temperature raised higher
As even if I were clothed from neck to toe in bad attire
You'd still be torn at which curves to observe, don't be a liar

Yes, I make sure I look very nice, but I don't do it to entice
Head held high with self-pride and wear whatever I like
You say I'm wrong to scold you with my hurtful truth and will
But vulgar lustful comments were the words you choose to spill

Thinking I would be so charmed and play along those lines
You obviously don't show respect or love for womankind
A different perspective shouldn't make you crass and rude
For if you only feel your dick, you'll be the one to lose

Tall, small, thick or thin, long hair, short or even bald
Shouldn't matter how we look upon your arm to all
Please listen very close and try to feel with a pure heart
Eyes should look straight into mine, not fixed on body parts

We know good looks and shapely figures in time will surely go
But hearts of deepest love will stay together and grow old
So be very careful what you wish the woman for you to be
As life will give you what you want, refunds on hearts aren't free

FACE THE TRUTH

I feel very trapped in a cage of my own making
I try to unlock my prison but shake with fear key in hand

Sometimes I hold my breath hoping for stillness to come
Suddenly I grasp for air and then the silent nightmare continues

I want to break free of the chains that hold me down
But terrified it is so deeply buried within my DNA

I try to be still and gently blow away the rising anxiety taking hold
I lay in bed frozen until its torturous grip subsides

When it does, I am left with numbness
Empty, until it's time to ride the tidal wave again

This storm I weather, time and time again
Wishing I could only stop the internal pain once and for all

This depth of despair I would not wish on my worst enemy
I realise now that it is my own reflection in the mirror

WHO WAS IT?

Who was it that turned my heart cold and mind blank?
So as to not remember the pain I suppressed deep within

Was it the time that neighbour pinned me against the wall
Wanting me to be scared and not push him away?

Or maybe it was the pervert in the car
Who stopped to ask directions while he masturbated?

I don't know. It could have been the monster on the bus
Who secretly fondled my breast whilst I sat frozen in shock?

Could have been the workman in our house, touching my thigh
Saying my leg started here, while he joked and ate his sandwich

Might have been the guy in a strange town, who offered me a lift,
Then drove me to his house and tried to force me to kiss him

Or my first boyfriend who couldn't handle our relationship issues,
Then betrayed me by going with another girl more experienced

Sometimes I think, it may have been the many occasions men
Verbally abused, embarrassed or harassed me in the street

Most probably it was the lies and deceit my close relative told,
When he molested me and disguised it as helping my ailment

I know it happened long before that vile narcissistic creature,
Seduced me into having sex, and then violently raped me all night

Whoever it was, I will no longer allow them to cause me pain,
I am a survivor, not a victim; I now take back my control and power

I HOPE TO SEE YOUR FACE AGAIN

You were so brave to face the fear
To know your end was very near
No time to really take it all in
Inside your head a panic spins

Exterior you were surreal
Beautiful words you said in still
To reassure your darling mate
Love you, my children in God's sake

Although your pain not fully clear
Felt helplessness so hard to bear
For everything around a mess
Yet keeping others from distress

You badly wished it wasn't so
Knew quick, would be the way you'd go
Emotional whirlwind inside
I wonder how you managed to hide

Reciting your last known words
Felt inner trauma as I heard
The sentiment in which they were said
Oh how I wish you weren't dead

Forever remembered worldwide
All victims of the hateful crime
That day imprinted on our brain
We pray all never died in vain

In memory of Cee Cee Lyles
Flight Attendant on the fatal 9/11 United Airlines 93 flight
http://www.youtube.com/watch?v=LiX7mNV4ab0

THE MASK

I mask the pain I feel inside
With a big bright smile on the outside
To show I am the same as others
When I truly know I am not

I laugh and joke and seem so happy
Sometimes I even convince myself
But really feel the bitter sadness
That makes me want to choke

There is a numbness of the brain
Loss of time and a confusion of self
Constantly wanting to pull up and out
Of the drowning from the mental load

You are you, but not yourself
A stranger invading your mind
As if you're cloned with a slight glitch
The tiny speck of you screaming help

Fighting for release and freedom
You walk in a foreign body
So strange but familiar all at once
Hoping people don't see the replica

Functioning like a robot daily
Almost wishing you could end it all
And be free from the nothingness
But you strive on with a slither of hope

THE MISSING LINK

WOW! The heart of a woman must be really strong
To endure all that life throws in her pathway

Yet tender to care, love, nurture and cherish
Whilst carrying the weight of the world on her shoulders

The same world that claims to love her, but seems to also judge
Criticize so harshly, blame, abuse as well as mistrust

Is this the way you think she deserves to be treated?
The one that gave birth to all and held tight to her bosom

Only goes to show how very out of touch we all are
To make her cry sad tears of love for those who stone her

Be mindful of the words you speak and thoughts you think
Remember: Grandma, Mother, Sister, Daughter are the missing link

THE SHOW MUST GO ON

The reluctant actress
That is what I am
A leading role I play
In my pretend world

Exuding excellence and flare
Strong in character
I command the stage
Feeding the audience

Engaging, full of charm
I draw them all in
My voice intoxicating
With a smile and a laugh

When the lights go out
And the curtain falls
That's the real blackout
As the applause faintly dies

I can barely look at my reflection
When I take off each layer
The slow emerging of myself
My heart wound open wide

Look into my blank eyes
I cannot hold your gaze
For hidden excuses and lies
Of the empty feeling inside

My confidence slides away
The shy little girl appears
So I put on my mask
To camouflage amongst adults

The disguise I've worn so long
I hold tightly, but know won't last
Almost transparent and torn now
Time to face the music and dance

WALK STRAIGHT

Put down the knife, put down the gun
Do you really want to hurt someone?

Think of all the heartache it will cause
When you break the law and moral rules

Don't have to do it, just to prove you're big
Bigger if you take the righteous path to live

You want to fit in, be part of the crew
Think they got your back, if only you knew

How they laugh at you when turned away
Showed you got game, but it's a joke they play

Didn't want to do it, mug that mobile phone
Never saw you crying when you ran home

Shaking with adrenalin, the anger and fear
Triumph so short lived now guilt and despair

Could have been your sister, mother or aunt?
Have to rethink this and take a different stance

Do you have the courage to finally pull away?
Got to be a man, stand up and have your say

Challenging your peers is not an easy task
Man will shout and threaten your life won't last

Got to break away and make a total fresh start
Never looking back, that life now in your past

Will always catch you up, when you least expect
So walk good now, before you live in sorrow and regret

NO JUSTICE

Had your sickening playful fight
Each one of you with hate in sight
You were so cold and inhumane
Laughing hard at your murder game

The audacity at every turn
Walking free with no concern
Chest held high and smirk on face
People swear outcry disgrace

Hid the racist crime you done
Thought 'Guilty' would touch not one
But two of you are in the dock
For three, time's now a ticking clock

Standing up to face your peers
Head held strong, no shameful tears
Waiting for the judgement call
Courtroom silent, stay or fall

Hot off the press, 'Gets 15 Years'
It's no surprise, but not severe
For 18 long you all stayed free
Justice for Stephen Lawrence, Please!

WE CELEBRATE YOU

Devastating was the cost
Shocking is the heartfelt loss
Feel no more a solid ground
One so great should be shot down

Took for granted everyday
You'd be there to always say
What the world needed to hear
So mesmerising was your steer

Callous was your sad defeat
Now people fighting in the streets
The coward way displayed the loathe
Of peaceful words in which you clothed

Your penetration did run deep
No longer do our people sleep
But now they fight with fist in air
Justice for murder so unfair

You were fearless in your cause
Equality you spoke for all
Stood head high broke all rules
For that I give hearty applauds

We never thought that one so great
Would take our heavy load and state
To conquer everyone it seems
With touching words 'I have a dream'

You did not die in total vain
We never will forget the pain
Don't underestimate our past
One day we will say 'Free at last!

STOP SPREADING THE HATE

Am I too open with my feelings?
I try to stay true to my heart
But wonder if I give too much
Laughing loud and speaking my mind

Expressing myself seems to unsettle people
Makes them uncomfortable, they think I'm over the top
Not real, or just pretending and seeking attention
I refuse to take in their hatred and jealousy

What do you expect from me?
To be fake and on your negative level
Oh, how I dread to be that shallow
Don't care what you all think of me

No, I don't want to talk about her
Or know what latest fashions are in
Who's dating who, or suing who
They call it gossip, I call it bullying

We all say we're against it
But still the media promotes it
Like a never ending sick joke
We laugh at it like addicts

Shame on us, for not supporting
Standing up and saying no to the ridicule
Judging those you don't even know
Just because they're in the public eye

Always speak with kind loving words
Without fear of isolation for doing so
Don't think your view isn't of value
Because they're not of the majority

Nobody knows how it feels to be that person
On the receiving end of the insults and lies
Until you can really truly know a person
Do not voice you invalid opinion of them

THE DELIVERY

Did not believe my woe and cries
Of the hurt I felt inside
"No! You're not in labour now,
You'll have to bear the pain somehow."

So tortuous it was so strong
Feeling as if I don't belong
Twisting and turning panic faced
My heart beating a frantic pace

I crunch on ice, I don't want tea
The melting water soothing me
Distracting from contraction waves
So gripping I'm a helpless slave

Reluctantly I do declare
The feeling of the baby near
But I'm ignored and hear them say
"Only her first, leave her to stay"

Just because my cries are low
And not full decibel I blow
You don't believe I am for real
The constant battering I feel

In disbelief I raise myself
And hold onto the nurse's shelf
To try to walk and leave the ward
My birth partner I now must call

I struggle back but door is locked
Is this for real? I am in shock
Nurse opens door, I am unseen
No questions of where have I been?

She walks off mumbling to self
"For goodness sake, God help my health!
Forgot what I was doing now,
Will have to remember somehow."

Once again I press the bell
Oh please release me from this hell
The monitor strap is very tight
They don't care think my hurt is slight

"The baby's heartbeat normal, see!
Now quiet down and leave it be.
Delivery room we could take you
But you'll just return to start anew."

"Alright, alright if you insist
Let's wheelchair you then take the lift."
My sister then thank God arrives
To hold my hand and smile with pride

We enter in the delivery suite
Midwife seems kind and so upbeat
Prepares me first for gas and air
Then says, "Now let me check down there."

The panic in her eyes and face
Sensing this, a difficult case
"Oh My God I do declare,
Press that button the baby's here!"

"You're fully crowned, the head's right there!
Push hard the pain you now must bear.
Deep breath and try with all your might."
But what I felt gave me a fright

The tightening stretch between my legs
"Forgive me, Lord." I have to beg
I pray for all under the Sun
I even shout out "Oh God Mum."

"You're doing well", the midwife says
My sister grins and strokes my head
Mum always said this pain is ripe
She never lied, it's out of sight

I feel like I'm a little lemon
Squeezing out a watermelon
And that was only just the head
The limbs and shoulders I do dread

My baby boy delivered fast
I know love will forever last
Mother and child both in good health
Give thanks I hold his joyous wealth

YOUNG PRINCE WEAR YOUR CROWN

Stay strong young Prince, stay strong
I know the road is hard and long
You feel you've lost control and will crash and burn
With the sheer volume of work you have to wade through

Questioning is it worth all the sacrifice in the end
Only you can answer that question to your dream
For it has been your vision for so long to achieve this goal
Never contemplated the intensity of focus it would take

Young Prince you know deep down you can walk this
Must concentrate fully on the task at hand 100%
Every day with each step you take you are closer
To reaching your target, only visualise the end result

Hold your head high; be proud of yourself as we are of you
You must know you're looked up to and are very much loved
By elders who trust they can leave our world in your good hands
Also by the youngsters hoping that you will also path their way

For you hold the key and lead our future plans of success
By the royal example you set in your thoughts, words and actions
Stay true and loyal to the royal status which is your duty to claim
Rightfully yours but was so inhumanly taken from your psyche

Know yourself well, so there is no doubt of what you can do
Once you align with your greatness the realm is limitless
Look upwards dear Prince and don't be afraid to fly high
Wear your crown with great pride and it will never fall again

I AM NOT

I am not stupid,

I am not my mistakes,

I am not your guilt,

I am not a victim,

I am not my abusers,

I am not my frienemies,

I am not a liar,

I am not unworthy,

I am not selfish,

I am not a hypocrite,

I am not judgmental,

I am not jealous,

I am not hateful,

I am not ugly,

I am not unforgiving,

I am uniquely ME!

PASS IT ON

I must share my work
For it was given for a purpose
Whether it is clear to me or not
Definitely not meant for hiding

When you have knowledge
Something of value to say
Give or service to render
So it must be distributed to all

Always pass it on
We are here not alone
But as one in each other
And in the living Universe

Let it be that we prosper
To dwell in total love energy
That was meant from time
Burning never-ending bright

Hotter than the sun is the gift
Life of bliss and joyous laughter
Holding hands together unified
Tears roll down my cheek in elation

How I wish I no longer imagine
But witness the coming to fruition
Strengthen me in your vigour
For contributing to the cause

SLIMSPIRATION ♥ PART 3

*"You do not have to see the whole staircase,
just take the first step."*

Dr. Martin Luther King. Jr.
1929–1968

The Awakening

After several previous attempts at losing weight, I vowed never again. I was afraid of yet another failure, but I so wanted to be slim and at last live a full healthy life. My son was now a teenager and would soon be going college. After all these years, I finally realised it was time to put ME first.

Sick and tired of fighting my bouts of depression, I wondered why my life was this way. Questions flooded my mind but I had no answers and no one to turn to. It's hard to describe the wonderment of what happened to me next, but I can honestly say I felt my soul spirit energy reciting words to me, whispered from the Universe. I never was a good sleeper, but now my head was consumed with thousands of thoughts and feelings that seemed to overtake my mind, until I had to release them. I would jump out of bed as I thought my head would explode if I never recorded the transcript as given. I was used to writing songs but this was something new, verses of words with no accompanying melody. Some so touchingly beautiful, that my heart wept with pure gratitude. It was January 2012 and I sensed a shift in the air. I felt lighter and happier at this new found uplift. The only thing weighing me down was my heavy frame, now dress size 24 and 36L cup bra. I never weighed myself, but guessed I must've been around 16 stones. This was extreme and morbidly obese for my small height of 5'4".

I remember watching amazing weight loss transformation videos online for almost two years. Longing, I too would glowingly be happy, showing off my before and after photos. I liked the YouTube channel and joined their Facebook group. It was New Year's Eve 2011/12 when I received a surprise phone call. The male voice on the other end said, 'Let me help you change your life!' His name was

Laurence Brown, the consultancy he ran with his partner Sharon Myrie, was Dual Dynamics. They were the top of their field with the Cambridge Weight Loss Plan. (CWP) Even after that first call, it still took me eight months to take the plunge and go for it 100%.

I was nervous at meeting the legendary Laurence Brown at my first consultation. He was passionate about helping people and had a stern no nonsense approach. His excitable personality was infectious and his partner Sharon was a beautiful dynamite Queen who pulled no punches. They showed so much belief in me and knew I could do the program to great success. To me, they were like superheroes and soon became dear friends. The scales shouted an unforgiving 15st at me, and I was told my goal weight was 9st 7lbs.

I started on Step 1: Sole Source, which meant total meal replacement. I wanted to make a drastic change and this certainly was that. The program entailed consuming high protein products, forcing your body to use its own fat for extra energy. This was scientifically known as setting your body into ketosis. My instructions were to; replace all three meals a day with these specially formulated packet foods and drink 3 – 4 litres of water. That was it, and then move up the steps. Slowly increasing calories and adding different food groups. Like a very long version of weaning a baby from liquids to solids. It made sense and was exactly what I needed, a complete rebirth.

From the very first meal, I couldn't believe how good all the products tasted. Days 1–3 were the hardest as my body adjusted to the minimal intake of calorie and carbohydrates. I was determined to get through that first week, (as if I could manage that) I knew all I had to do was repeat the process. It was like a miracle, I found a totally focused mindset I never even knew was in me. On day five, I was serving food for 120 people at my sister's surprise 50th Birthday party. Not once did I deviate from the plan. By day seven, I was euphoric at completing the first week and losing an astonishing 5lbs. That high remained throughout my whole journey. I started to believe I was worthy and deserved to live a happy healthy life. My perspective changed and I gradually felt a new found love and respect for myself. It may sound strange that changing your diet could do that, but it did.

The weeks went quickly and the weight was melting off. By the second month people really noticed the difference. Surprisingly, some were not so happy with my new shrinking figure. There were only a handful of people fully behind me whilst dieting. It showed me how many flaky people and frienemies were in my life. I didn't care what anyone thought, I was on a mission. My solid as a rock consultants and new found mindset was the biggest supporting factor towards my transforming body and life.

By month four, I was over half way and could see the end in sight. I felt so proud and truly grateful to find patience and appreciation for every humble experience along the way. The little things like; thighs not chafing, a standard size bath towel wrapping around me, and for the first time actually seeing my crossed arms under my smaller bust. Another amazing health benefit was my doctor reducing my tablets, until I was completely off all medication. My blood sugar levels were now in the normal range as a non-diabetic.

Whilst in my focused diet bubble, life still went on with all its wonderful highs and sometimes devastating lows. November was the worse time for me. The walls in every room of my house were stripped to the brickwork, to repair gapping cracks from severe subsidence. Pure dust everywhere, it was like living on a building site, but I still managed my diet plan. Then my father was admitted to hospital because of complications with his failing kidneys. Within two weeks, I watched him take his last breath.

They say that God never gives you more than you can cope with, and you never know how strong you are until faced with adversity. I was astonished at my resilience even when emotionally drained. My focus was stronger than ever and I didn't eat one crumb throughout all my grieving. I know my dad would have been proud. He never liked a quitter and I was determined not to be one, in honour or his memory.

I continued on to surpass my goal weight of 9st 7lbs, to become a size 8/10 at 9st 3lbs. I had photo shoots, a magazine article and best of all; my own YouTube success story video. (https://youtu.be/vZor8erFGtA) It took seven months to lose 5st 10lbs. I loved my new slender petite frame and felt on top of the world. Eight months later, I was shortlisted for CWP Slimmer of the Year. I attended the Convention as a V.I.P guest. I never won, but in my mind I was a successful winner from Day 1.

When you really want something and decide to love yourself enough to achieve it, you will always give your 100% best. I've learnt to love and believe in myself much more and that absolutely anything is possible, once you commit to your end goal. Just Believe!

Chapter 3:
Rise

Reflection Empowerment Rebirth
Let your full greatness shine

I AM THE MESSENGER

I am the messenger, please know and remember
The world needs you, you are so important

As earth spins around the sun and the trees grow leaves
You are part of the cycle that keeps life turning daily

Would not be the same time and place without you in it
For you are part of the equation, everything connected

We may not see, feel or believe it at times, but it is so
Each living thing has a vibration, one pulse in sync

Many close their eyes or are unaware of the joining thread
Invisible to the love we share, they are blinded by hard hearts

Sometimes lost and unappreciative of the beautiful blessings
Stay true to self and spread the joy of love to all living things

Do not have doubt or question your value on this earth plane
For you are here for a purpose, reach within yourself to find it

The true reason you exist, you are here for but a short time
Great is the journey you have taken to be among each other

Spread love as wide and deep as the sea, climb the mountains high
To the summit, spread your angel wings then take off beyond the stars

It is not at trick of the mind or our imagination that dreams of this
The power within us is so great we in fact have not limitations

We are not human, but super human as this is just our earth shell
More incredible than any action packed special effects feature film

Be in awe of yourself and the wonderfulness you bring in just being
Blessed are we to roam this planet, before we return to our true form

EMPTY THE TRASH

The surrounding clutter is slowly killing you
Brain numbing, clogs your mind of its clarity

Everywhere you look something fills the spot
Crowding space, movement and the psyche

You always tell yourself, "I'll clear that up later"
When you fully know that later never seems to come

The unreachable tomorrow we forever chase
Which runs as if not wanting to be captured

Like a child playing in the summer sun
Trying to catch moving shadows on the ground

It is not promised nor belongs to anyone
For unfortunately it doesn't come to us all

Always there but never really seems to arrive
For it's the now we should live in day to day

Must be a reflection of the mind state
Forever distracted and putting things off

Silence it from the constant unnecessary chatter
And the insignificant oddities that accumulates

Overwhelmed at what seems a vast never-ending task
Just try starting with a little at a time, bit by bit

It may take a while, but clearness gradually appears
Leaving you free to receive your true life message

I AM WORTHY

I'll try to forgive you; I'll try to forgive me
For allowing the subtle overtaking of my will
Loving myself so little for far too long
I put you and others before me

So wanted to be accepted and loved by you
With your magnificent confidence and shine
Wishing I too would have such radiance
By being with your vivacious personality

I was wrong to put you on a pedestal
Loved you so, felt grateful for such a friend at my side
But slowly began to realise something wasn't right
It was in fact I, who shone so brightly in people's eyes

You were merely magnified by the attention I drew
Illuminated by my presence in your company
Unaware of this by my insecurities from years of abuse
Was always my normality, didn't recognise your stronghold

Eager to please, willingly open to change myself
To live up to your suiting whenever you needed me to
Dumbstruck at the light bulb moment, not an equal friendship
No. So needy of love, I was blind to the unnatural imbalance

Yes. I stood by you through thick and thin at all times
Laughter and tears, struggles and triumphs every step
But I now admit defeat to true love, the love of self
Given by the one, our everlasting first love, the Creator

He has led me to finally see that my true worth resides within
Which has in turn, shown me that you are not worthy of it
So as much as I have loved you deeply dear friend
I now have to love myself even more, right to my core

If or whenever you are ready to accept me unconditionally
I hope I will have strength and courage with an open heart
For true forgiveness to maybe receive you again. But until then,
I must walk away with no regrets and head high knowing
I gave my all

HEAL THE WOUND

Yes! At last! Comfortable in my skin
I have no need to justify my being
Always compromising trying to please
That desire for acceptance forever gone

When you have hurt in your heart
From the very ones that made you
It is a deep rooted soul piercing agony
Sometimes beyond even earthly repair

Having the courage to face your demons
Maybe even yourself, is no easy task
Unreasonable to consider forgiveness
So broken is the wound in your fragile soul

Within the pain that surrounds you
There is a small voice crying to be heard
Calling you back to the love that is yours
Allow it to resonate and fill your emptiness

For it is your true self fighting for forgiveness
Of wrong done unto you by others but more so
By you for continually permitting the hurt to fester
The hardest thing to recognise and accept

Move forward in your new coat of confidence
Knowing that it is now you that sets the pace
With a higher understanding of self-residing
Penetrate and emitting positive energy alone

RETURN TO SPLENDOR

I am ready to meet my higher self
Starting again from the beginning

Feeding body with essential nutrients
Purifying water quenching my thirst

Mind on positivity overdrive
Determined to reach my goal

No more in the darkness
I step into the light renewed

Born again like God intended
Perfect in every way possible

Humble thanks I give in honor
Of the one divine for creating me

I will strive to remain the angelic child
You rose with love in your heart

Now I recognise and accept that love
Within myself that no man can dissolve

Knowing I have the tools you gave
To stand strong and be my true self

With kind loving graciousness
Respecting others as I do myself

I bow my head to you in tribute
Receive my crown in your glory

Let it be now and forever more
The manifestation of abundance

ACCEPT YOUR PURPOSE

Can't find the words to explain
How vulnerable my heart feels right now
As if it would burst from the pure happiness I feel

Only words I can use to describe it
Is to say I am on the edge of ecstasy
Wanting to taste its full beauty
But too afraid to take that leap

Wanting something with all your might
So compelled by the sheer intent
Its grip holding 'til I'm exhausted and confused
With the decision to excel or remain the same

Too much of a change when so used to just being
In such a lethargic fashion
Subdued with procrastination
Everything in slow motion almost in reverse

Take the next step towards the light
It is now your calling, your time to shine
Held back for way too long now
Only you can make that initial step

Do so with true passion and determination
That no other can knock you off your course
Have faith and believe this is right
Only you hold the key to your own destiny

No one else can walk in your shoes
Or choose what is meant only for you
Your part is crucial, in line with the universe
As without your existence, a different time unfolds

Not insignificant as you first thought
But mighty like the force of the elements
To the core source of life itself
You remain the prize jewel in every crown

Rise to the glory, your ceremony overdue
Essential for you to take your seat at the throne
Imminent is your carnation no time to lose
If now you are not ready, another day you'll choose

HAPPY TO TOTALLY LOVE ME FIRST

I keep myself free
from the physical love I crave
Helps me not to lose focus
on my true heart's desire
To have a deep meaning soulful love
right to my spirit core

Not to say I don't sometimes have
the urge to break my fast
For I am naturally a red
blooded woman with needs
Who still has a high drive
and a vivid imagination too

However, I feel it necessary
to quench that thirst in other ways
As I want to wait for the right one
and time to share my pride
One who is worthy to give myself fully
and wholeheartedly to

Don't think I am the only woman
who believes in this or lives this way
We are many, with years of living
without any delusion, shame or guilt
Some of us by choice, some not so
but accepting the way it is for now

You may think I'm a fool to not want
to experience that part of life

But I think it foolish to waste
your true essence for a fleeting moment
Means more to me to have a pure
spiritual bond before a physical love

Everyone to their own choices,
I respect yours without judgement
The same as I would expect you
to respect mine without prejudice
Even if you don't, let's just agree
to disagree and live and let live

I'm no better than you for not doing so,
nor you lesser than me for so doing
It is a personal decision I feel comfortable with
at this time in my life
Maybe one day I'll throw caution to the wind
and just give of myself freely

In a world so saturated with sexual imagery,
I find my abstinence soothing
Giving me clarity of mind and soul,
releasing overload of negative emotions
Don't feel pressured to fill the so-called 'void'
with other stimulant substances

Until that day comes, I take pleasure
in the pleasing comfort I have alone
You can say; it's not meant to be that way,
it's selfish, unnatural even immoral
But I am happy to live my life this way,
I hope you can say the same of yours

SAVE OURSELVES

Why do people always try to steal your joy?
Shading your shinny star like brightness
They criticize and cut you down like a tree
So deep in their self-loathing and jealousy

Why does it pain them so that you glow?
Illuminating others as you pass by
Your aura mesmerizing their hearts
Enchanting them deep within the soul

Why do we make assumptions?
That others are not great or worthy
Prejudging from no prior knowledge
Imagination painting a whole new story

Where is the humanity and compassion?
The innocence that was once within us
Wholeness and purity from which we were born
Unconditional gentleness and loving for each other

This harsh cold world has contaminated the spirit
Senseless is the bitter cruelty we inflict upon ourselves
Painful is the lost humility given way to arrogant pride
Empathy gone for those we see as weak and hopeless

Where are the days that children were safe to play outside?
Interacting with joy and laughter at the fun filled adventure
Now in the gadgets and gizmos that separates and detach us
So many view and believe the reality of media and TV

Aching sadness I feel to these stark realizations
Surrendered to greed, lies, hatred, ego and injustice
Wondering how long we have before self-destruction
Or earth crumbles from our constant violent bruising

Why have we forgotten our superior intelligence?
Is this really how far we have come in all these years?
Surely this is not all there is after our long journey
How many reincarnations will it take to learn the lesson?

SHIFTING

Strike while the iron is hot
Do not lose the plot
Create the world you wish
The way to Universal bliss

You can make it a reality
Just have to start with one
Then multiply by double score
The world you seek will be assured

So do it now before you wane
And life revolves to lesser plane
For not long will you have the gift
Of insight so direct to source

Ferocious force is needed now
Cannot contain in mind only
Intensifying is the seeing
And overwhelm is of extreme

A new beginning is for all
The choice is ours, pray do not fall
Awakening is rarely here
So grasp the light and hold it dear

The shower of a love supreme
Will reign forever not a dream
Foresight yours a birthright gift
So don't delay just make the shift

TO LOVE AGAIN

I see your pain, the hurt inside
From so deep, your face cannot hide
You joke around without a world's care
All the while growing in dark despair

Always keeping up the pretence
Your life almost a prison sentence
Overtaken with such sadness and guilt
Knowing your love was so carelessly spilt

Many years you took the loneliness to heart
Feeling so wronged with the decision to part
Thought this time, the one, was in your grasp
Never contemplated someday it wouldn't last

You vowed to never open yourself to love again
The wound so deep still drives you insane
A constant battle the yo-yo game you daily play
"Shall I open up to give my broken heart away?"

Never fully comfortable when feelings do attract
Yes you'll take the offer, but a soulful love you lack
If only had the courage to put hurt feelings aside
Reward would be fulfilling, an overflow of pride

DON'T OPEN THE BOX

It wouldn't hurt to have a few
You thought, but never had a clue
One bite and then you ate the lot
Just like an addict, couldn't stop

The luscious taste within your mouth
That joyous feeling, pigging out
All worries seem to melt away
No thinking of the bills to pay

You tell yourself 'Been good all week!'
And 'You deserve a special treat'
But one became, two, three plus four
Until you couldn't keep up score

And when you think you've had your fill
The food seems to take your free will
You try to fight, but still eat blind
To fuel the hunger in your mind

You start to think it's all too late
You've eaten this enormous plate
And surely you'll tip every scale
A balance that will leave you pale

Deep down you knew it wasn't right
Ignored your stomach feeling tight
Squeezing as much into your mouth
Forgetting all will come out South

The more and more you stuff your face
Eventually you'll feel disgrace
The pleasure doesn't last for long
And soon you'll sing the 'Sorry Song'

Of guilt and constant self-hate talk
Punishment for the road you walked
That record you now know must change
New healthy life to rearrange

You've heard it said 'It's no long ting'
And know 'no stories' you must bring
So do the maths, don't muck about
4 litres of water, products, out!

You got to know your Platinum goal
And step into your greatness whole
To stay on plan and lose the weight
And maintain your new slimmer waist

Road may be long or short to go
Whatever, there'll be highs and lows
But know it's you who chose your fate
A life of less or one that's great

You're not alone, we are a team
Supporting one another's dream
Setting the pace, challenges met
You sealed the deal, laid down your bet

But up to you and no one else
The hard or easy route to self
The true person you know is inside
Time to reveal no longer hide

The real you you're destined to be
Where all your doubts and fears just flee
Never to visit your old scars
But reach up high beyond the stars

RESET REFINED

Stop giving it away, stop giving it away
Don't think that it is rightfully yours
Always passing it on to others
The takers, ever ready to pounce

Freely give away the tools and gifts
Brought to your hand for you to use
Never thinking it was meant for you
Putting loved ones first instead

Many years you wasted this way?
Not feeling confident, less in esteem
So sinful, the disbelief in yourself
Contamination stilled your growth

Restore the original setting anew
Regain the path already set for you
When in alignment with the chosen plan
Your glory will now forever expand

FORGIVING LOVE

I am cleansing my body, mind and soul
To once again return myself to whole
In the pure beauty of loving forgiveness

Like a new rising dawn, I awaken fresh
Releasing any negative toxins of yesterday
It does not serve any purpose in my now

As it is a dead weight that stifles life
Restricts your growth and acceptance
Of totally loving your wonderful divine self

It is within you to really be who you truly are
Without any contaminating mind control
From things that do not support you in this world

Make the decision to stop the constant self-loathing
This repetitive behaviour eats away at your soul
Open your eyes to the internal damage you inflict

Free your ears and listen to your inner God voice
Crying out for you to hear its true peaceful call
Of beautiful love, forgiveness and humble gratitude

Fully acknowledge the blessings in your life
For although at times it feels you may have none
Look with your heart and be surprised at how many

You have always deserved the very best in life
That is what we are meant to experience here
An abundance of joyous laughter with no pain

Spreading your infectious love deep and wide
To every living being until nothing is untouched
In the core spirit of glorious universal oneness

THE DIVINE IN YOU

The time has come
To fully recognise
Who you really are

Ever growing
To the expansion
You are limitless

Developing each day
Rising with courage
Evolving creatively

Do not let soul suckers
Spoon feed you filth
To digest negativity

They are rife with envy
Slowly draining you
Of your pure heart

Wear precious love
Your security shield
To repel wickedness

The Divine in you
Is your amour
For you are sacred

At every turn
You are blessed
Of highest Royalty

Never forget
With whom you reside
Universal love child

WITH BREATH OF LIFE

Grateful for the sun
Thankful another day begun

Have breath in my bones
Not laying cold for a tombstone

Alive one more day
To spread laughter, love, joy and play

Not giving up hope
Knowing through struggles I will cope

Sharing my true art
I give to others with full heart

With a beat so strong
Determination never gone

I raise high my game
To take a chance and not complain

Looking for the day
Together in one love we pray

YOU WILL RISE AGAIN

It's scary sometimes when you start to feel this way
Alone, like you're the only one in the whole world
Your mind seems to be playing tricks on you
Emotions up and down wondering will you ever feel right

Standing in the garden of two entirely different worlds
As if each in separate seasons of time and space
Lost in the loneliness of life, you search for the meaning
But can you ever be sure you are on the right path

Doubting, you struggle to maintain normality in every day
Only the power of prayer stops you from going over the edge
Hard to keep faith with tremendous hatred and evil everywhere
You must be strong, deep within you know goodness will prevail

When you are down, low and in the valley of depression
It's easy to just lay there and let it completely consume you
Take courage and just know you will not feel this way for long
As when you are down, the only possible way now is to rise up

Stand with pride as you take each day at a time to gather strength
You cannot go back to the negative place which serves no purpose
Do not wallow in self-pity as it may take you on a destructive path
If you fall again, you know you can get up as you've done before

You can do it, you have to, by whatever means it takes
Find a way, or are you gonna just give up on yourself?
Life goes on whether you want to be a part of it or not
Please don't give up, believe anything is possible and try

The first few steps are the hardest, but you first have to take them
You may feel afraid but let that fear be your drive to something positive
You feel the fear anyway, so why not, what's the worst that can happen?
Oh, you might fall down again. Well you know the answer to that.
Get up!

A NEW LIFE

Out with the old, in with the new
Time for a fresh start
A different coat I will now wear, one to
Rejuvenate, motivate and inspire me

For I have come to the conclusion
I cannot aspire to my life's true potential
Without the right attitude, mindset and focus
Passion with determination will bring success

It is scary to step out of the comfort zone
Asking myself if I'm really happy with my life?
Or just settling for medico run of the mill
An existence so stagnant no room for growth

Yes, the road ahead is long, but I'm ready to run
Full throttle to achieve my goals
Ticking them off the list one by one
Giving thanks and gratitude with each completed

Helps me to make new dreams come alive
Reviving the soul to its uppermost realm
Contentment beyond measure so overjoyed
Life capturing true essence of a loving world

LET THE HEALING BEGIN

I detach myself from the pain
The pain that once gripped me so tightly
Stifling me psychologically
And held me in an emotional childlike state

I let out the cry loud and strong
And exhaust the silent scream I muffled inside so long
You can block your ears not wanting to hear if you wish
But the imprisoned hurt from my soul must be released

Many will be shocked and may refuse to believe me
Or cast the stone of judgement, blame and guilt
The fact is, no one has lived in my head or walked in my shoes
But however people respond to the revelations, it's my history

And that's where it will remain, in the past
For I am hopeful and looking into my bright future
I can forgive the past but will not forget the trauma
As still part of me and has brought me to this present day

That is the precious gift I will at last allow myself
The joy of a renewed life finally at peace
Accepting and loving who I am
And who I am evolving to become

For I am certain only positivity will be my outcome
Standing proud with head once again held high
Spreading the word of permission to speak
A platform of openness for the broken adult child within

Stop rewinding past events that cloud your mind
Time to let go and move away from your achingly bruised heart
For if you do not face the fear of what you buried so deeply
You only continue the abuse leading your own self destruction

So let the road to complete soul healing begin
It may be long with some congestion, breakdowns and delays
But your journey will eventually reach the destination
Of whatever your true desire and life purpose holds

JUMP

Even when you think you have given your all
There is still more inside that you can give
For you have an insurmountable store within
What we are capable of is truly beyond our wildest dreams

Take courage to really pursue your goals to fruition
Only you can make that choice of fight or flight
When fear has got you thinking you are not able
Your intuition will tell you to take the challenge

Always tell yourself you can
Say it out loud if you have to
Better to hear the words from your own mouth
So your ears can tell your brain what it hears is true

Repeat daily, for the dose is prescribed as your medicine
If you don't believe you can do it, others won't either
Convincing yourself is the first hurdle to jump
But once you do, you'll be surprised how high you can

GODDESSNESS

I'm learning to trust and accept
The Goddess in me
Gradually starting to realise
I am worthy to be

For the world so cruelly
Dispelled it from my psyche
I did not even recognise
The shadow of my lesser self

Expanding vision to infinity
I rise fully crowned
Among my sister Goddess Angels
Harmoniously one in spirit and sound

We ascend serving our children
Giving to the mother earth
Richness of deep purple
Sumptuous and vast

Precious blessings we bestow
Sprinkled lightly with crystals
Of purest clarity
To awaken the inner God soul

Listen to the yearning
Evolve into your true self
DNA transforming
Everlasting love energy

EXPANSION

I am expanding ever more
Totaling on every score
Reaching for my every goal
Achieving it as best I know

Something so deep and rich inside
In keeping with my honor pride
Has magnified extremely high
Beyond the universal sky

Receiving gifts of which I dreamed
Once was in doubt but faith redeemed
I asked so it was given to
My life forever growing new

I humbly give thanks most great
For taking care filling my plate
You feed me well so now I'm strong
Praises, to thee I do belong

About the Author

Photo: David Mian

Jenessa is a single parent to one son and lives in London.

She initially trained as a dancer then changed direction and built a successful career as a singer.

A first class vocalist and Olivier Award winner, she has performed on the West End stage and with top artists in the music industry. She regularly tours Europe with her own gigs and in theatrical productions.

Jenessa is interested in raising awareness in support of women affected by the issues covered in her writing.

Her wish is to promote empowerment by elevating self-worth, confidence, love and healing. Through her poetry and speaking engagements, she hopes to provide a service of workshops in the near future.

Ingram Content Group UK Ltd.
Milton Keynes UK
UKHW020626070623
423009UK00006B/11

9 781912 551347